Washington, D.C.

Washington, D.C.

A Downtown America Book

Catherine Reef

ᴅP Dillon Press, Inc. Minneapolis, MN 55415

To my husband, John,
and my son, John Stephen

Photographic Acknowledgments

Photographs have been reproduced through the courtesy of Cameramann International (pages 10, 34, 37, 40, 54); Jessie Cohen, National Zoological Park; Joyce Garrett, Eastern High School; Kendrick Photography (pages 12, 13, 42, 49); Kiplinger Washington Collection (page 28); the Library of Congress; the National Archives; the National Park Service; Office of the Vice President; John W. Reef (pages 16, 19, 20, 22, 45, 47, 50, 51, 58, 61, 62); the U.S. House of Representatives; the Washington Redskins (page 18); and the White House. The photograph on page 30 copyright Washington Post; reprinted by permission of the D.C. Public Library. Cover photograph copyright National Geographic Society.

Library of Congress Cataloging-in-Publication Data

Reef, Catherine.
    Washington, D.C. / Catherine Reef.
        p.   cm. — (A Downtown America book)
    Includes index.
    Summary: Describes the past and present, neighborhoods, historic sites, attractions, and festivals of Washington, D.C.
    ISBN 0-87518-411-1 : $12.95
    1. Washington (D.C.)—Juvenile literature. [1. Washington (D.C.)] I. Title. II. Title: Washington, D.C. III. Series.
F194.3.R43 1990
975.3—dc20   89-12025
                                                                      CIP
                                                                       AC

Dillon Press, Inc., 242 Portland Avenue South
Minneapolis, Minnesota 55415

Printed in the United States of America
1 2 3 4 5 6 7 8 9 10 99 98 97 96 95 94 93 92 91 90

About the Author

Catherine Reef is a free-lance writer and editor who lives and works in the Washington, D.C., area. Currently, she is the editor of *Taking Care*, a monthly health education newsletter, and she has written many articles for adults on the subject of health. This is her first book for children.

Ms. Reef received her bachelor's degree in English from Washington State University. She is married and has one child.

Contents

Fast Facts about Washington, D.C.

Washington, D.C.: The nation's capital

Location: Southeastern United States, almost midway along the Atlantic coast, between Maryland and Virginia. Washington is located in the District of Columbia, a federal district that is not part of any state.

Area: City, 69 square miles (179 square kilometers); consolidated metropolitan area, 3,957 square miles (10,240 square kilometers)

Population (1987 estimates*): City, 622,000; consolidated metropolitan area, 3,646,000

Major Population Groups: Blacks, Hispanics, Asians

Altitude: Highest—410 feet (125 meters) above sea level; lowest—1 foot (.3 meter) above sea level

Climate: Average temperature is 37°F (3°C) in January, 78°F (26°C) in July; average annual precipitation, including rain and snow, is 41 inches (104 centimeters)

Founding Date: 1791; first housed the United States government in 1800

City Flag: The design for the Washington, D.C., flag was adapted from George Washington's family crest. Two horizontal red stripes run across a white background; centered above the stripes are three red stars.

City Seal: A female figure symbolizing justice stands beside a statue of George Washington. She holds a wreath in one hand and a stone tablet labeled "Constitution" in the other. To her left is the U.S. Capitol. The Potomac River, with the sun rising over the Virginia shore, can be seen in the distance.

Form of Government: Washington's mayor, the chief executive of the city government, is elected for a four-year term. The 13-member city council is responsible for making the city's laws. The U.S. Congress has certain powers in Washington's government, as well. The Congress can veto laws that the city council passes and can also pass its own laws affecting the city. The federal government pays no city taxes; instead, it

*U.S. Bureau of the Census 1988 population estimates available in fall 1989; official 1990 census figures available in 1991-92.

provides the city with a sum of money called the federal payment.

Important Industries: Government, tourism, high-technology firms, research and development

Festivals and Parades

January: Martin Luther King, Jr., Day Celebration

February: George Washington's Birthday Celebration and Parade; Abraham Lincoln's Birthday Ceremony at the Lincoln Memorial; Chinese New Year Festival; Black History Month

March: Saint Patrick's Day Parade; Smithsonian Kite Festival

March/April: White House Easter Egg Roll

April: National Cherry Blossom Festival and Parade; Imagination Celebration at the Kennedy Center; Thomas Jefferson's Birthday Ceremony at the Jefferson Memorial

May: Greek Spring Festival; Malcolm X Day; Memorial Day Wreath Laying at the Vietnam Veterans Memorial

June: Potomac Riverfest; Gay Pride Day Festival and Parade

June/July: Festival of American Folklife

July: Independence Day Celebration; Hispanic-American Culture Festival

September: National Frisbee Festival; Adams-Morgan Day; Constitution Day Commemoration at the National Archives

October: Capital City Jazz Festival; Neighborhood Halloween Celebrations at Georgetown and Dupont Circle

November: Veterans Day Ceremony and Service at Arlington National Cemetery

December: U.S. Capitol Tree Lighting; Pageant of Peace, including the Lighting of the National Christmas Tree; Smithsonian's Trees of Christmas Display

For further information about festivals and parades, see agency listed on page 67.

United States

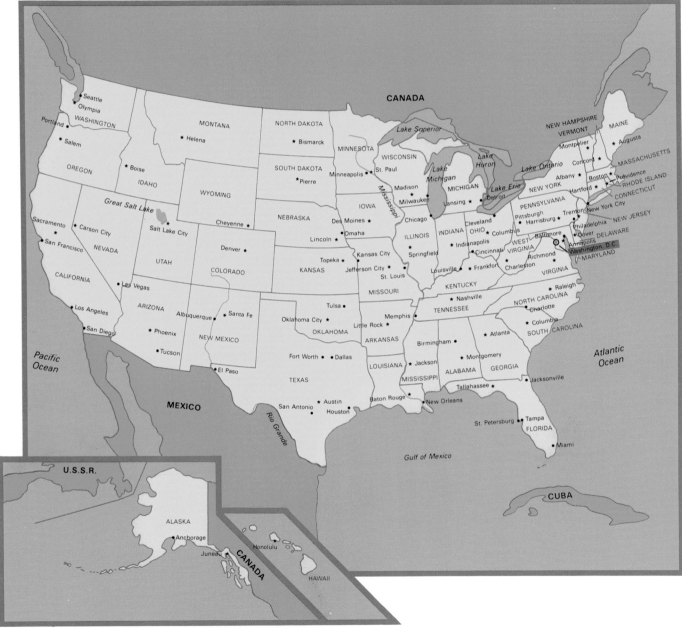

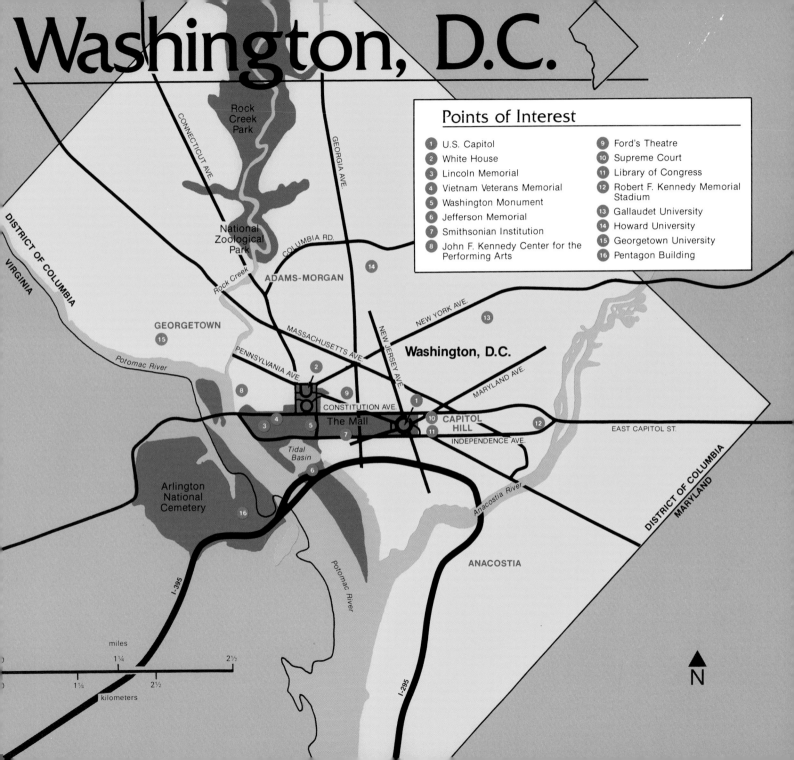

Washington, D.C.

Points of Interest

1. U.S. Capitol
2. White House
3. Lincoln Memorial
4. Vietnam Veterans Memorial
5. Washington Monument
6. Jefferson Memorial
7. Smithsonian Institution
8. John F. Kennedy Center for the Performing Arts
9. Ford's Theatre
10. Supreme Court
11. Library of Congress
12. Robert F. Kennedy Memorial Stadium
13. Gallaudet University
14. Howard University
15. Georgetown University
16. Pentagon Building

Washington, D.C.

Rock Creek Park

National Zoological Park

CONNECTICUT AVE.

GEORGIA AVE.

COLUMBIA RD.

ADAMS-MORGAN

Rock Creek

DISTRICT OF COLUMBIA

VIRGINIA

GEORGETOWN

Potomac River

MASSACHUSETTS AVE.

PENNSYLVANIA AVE.

NEW JERSEY AVE.

NEW YORK AVE.

MARYLAND AVE.

CONSTITUTION AVE.

The Mall

CAPITOL HILL

EAST CAPITOL ST.

INDEPENDENCE AVE.

Tidal Basin

Arlington National Cemetery

Anacostia River

Potomac River

ANACOSTIA

DISTRICT OF COLUMBIA

MARYLAND

I-395

I-295

miles

1¼

2½

1¼

2½

kilometers

N

1

A City for the People

More than any other American city, Washington, D.C., is in the public eye. This city leads two lives—one official, one private. Officially, it is the capital of the United States, the place where laws are made, where news happens, and where the president lives and works each day. In its private life, Washington is the home of about 622,000 Americans and the workplace of many thousands more.

Often visited and frequently photographed, the government's home makes a grand impression. Its wide, tree-lined avenues, white stone buildings, and delicate cherry blossoms are a source of pride for the American people. Many visitors come to the city to enjoy its beauty as they learn about U.S. government and history.

But Washington is more than a collection of monuments and historic

The U.S. Capitol, where the nation's laws are made, rises in the heart of Washington, D.C.

A statue of Thomas Jefferson, one of Washington's many historic sights.

buildings. It is a growing, changing city that can be crowded and noisy with people traveling to work and school. Washington is also an important center of culture, a place where people can watch parades, listen to concerts, and view the work of many artists.

Washington, D.C., is located near the middle of the Atlantic coast, between the states of Maryland and Virginia. It lies on the banks of two rivers, the Potomac River to the west and south, and the Anacostia River to the east. Here, winters are fairly mild, but summers are hot and humid. Most Washingtonians are pleased that heavy snows are uncommon, but when the thermometer reaches the upper 90s, and moisture

Many Washingtonians enjoy sailing or rowing on the Potomac River.

and air pollution turn the summer sky gray, almost everyone complains!

Washington is not part of any state. It is a separate capital district that was specially planned and built to house the United States government. The *D.C.* in Washington, D.C., stands for *District of Columbia.* The word *Columbia* comes from Christopher Columbus's name and is sometimes used to mean America.

Residents elect a mayor and a city council of 13 members to govern Washington, D.C., but the U.S. Congress controls much of the city's government. The Congress reviews Washington's budget, makes laws that affect the district, and sometimes vetoes, or strikes down, laws that the city council passes. Because the U.S.

government pays no taxes on its buildings and land, the Congress regularly gives the district a sum of money called the federal payment.

Even though it is a major city, Washington has been called a "company town"—a community where most people work for the same employer. In Washington, that employer is the United States government. More than one-third of the city's workers are government, or federal, employees. Having a government job usually means working in an office, but federal workers may perform a wide variety of tasks. Some answer telephones for busy senators, others print money or work to arrest criminals, and still others work for the post office.

Members of both houses of the U.S. Congress assemble in the Capitol.

Many other people work in Washington because they do business with the U.S. government offices in the city. These workers might have jobs with large companies, labor unions, law firms, or organizations such as the World Bank or the American Red Cross. Lobbyists work to get laws passed by the Congress that will favor the interests of various groups. Other Washington residents are actually citizens of other countries who represent foreign governments. They work in the stately

Visitors tour the Rotunda, the circular room underneath the dome of the Capitol.

mansions of Embassy Row.

Tourism is big business in Washington. Each year, more than 19 million people visit the city's monuments, museums, and government buildings, creating thousands of jobs for local residents in this growing industry.

Many Washingtonians work with visitors in restaurants, hotels, and gift shops. Vendors selling hot dogs, pretzels, T-shirts, and souvenirs labeled "Washington, D.C." line the busy downtown avenues.

Other Washington-area industries, such as the production of computer software, employ many people. The city is also known for its private research institutes, which often produce reports that affect public-policy decisions made by the Congress.

Many Washington children attend the city's public schools, while others study at one of the more than 75 private schools. Because the Washington area is growing, and because many jobs in the city require families to move often, Washington's young people are used to seeing schoolmates leave and new children enter their classes.

An older student can attend one of Washington's many outstanding universities. Georgetown University, founded in 1789, is the oldest U.S. college established by the Roman Catholic church. Howard University, one of the largest mostly black schools in the nation, offers a broad range of programs. The only U.S. college for the deaf, Gallaudet University, is also located in Washington.

When they are not working or attending school, the people of Washington have a wonderful opportunity to be tourists in their hometown. Residents often join out-of-town visitors in enjoying the city's many attractions: the Smithsonian Institution, the largest museum complex in the world; the dignified houses of government, including the White House and U.S. Capitol; and the memorials to past presidents and historical events.

Enthusiastic Washingtonians enjoy a Redskins football game.

Washingtonians might spend a day at the National Zoo, fly a kite near the Washington Monument, or ride an underground Metro train to Robert F. Kennedy Stadium to watch a Redskins football game or hear a rock concert. Every year, many of them visit the White House Christmas tree or watch the national fireworks display on the Fourth of July.

Celebrations such as these are an important part of city life. One of the best known is spring's week-long

These Washingtonians are taking part in a kite-flying festival near the base of the Washington Monument.

Vendors are common on Washington's bustling downtown streets.

Cherry Blossom Festival, which celebrates the blooming of Washington's many cherry trees. These trees surround the Tidal Basin, a lagoon near the Potomac River, and were a gift from the government of Japan.

As the Cherry Blossom Festival begins, a 300-year-old Japanese lantern is lit. The Japanese ambassador gives a speech of friendship; then, representatives of the U.S. government and the Washington city government speak. The week's special events include riverboat cruises, Japanese music, and the crowning of the Cherry Blossom Queen. The festival ends with a colorful parade viewed by many thousands of Washingtonians who line the street.

Most of Washington's citizens—

nearly 70 percent—are black, and many have moved to the city during the past 40 years. The city's Asian and Hispanic populations have also been growing. In recent years, immigrants from China, the Philippines, Korea, and many Central and South American countries have come to start a new life in the nation's capital.

Washington's people live in neighborhoods both old and new. Residents who like a bustling city atmosphere might live on busy streets close to stores and restaurants. Others prefer the city's quieter neighborhoods and houses with historic importance. Yet more and more people are choosing to make their homes in the suburbs in nearby Maryland and Virginia. Because many suburban residents drive to work, traffic tie-ups are a growing problem.

Still, wherever they live and whatever their heritage, Washingtonians share a deep pride in their city. The nation's capital is a place for people from every U.S. state and from countries around the world to visit, learn from, and enjoy.

2

Home to History

Visitors to Washington, D.C., can stand on the steps of the Lincoln Memorial, where the Reverend Martin Luther King, Jr., called for better treatment of blacks in his famous "I Have a Dream" speech. They can also tour Ford's Theatre, where President Abraham Lincoln was assassinated. In these moments, people may feel close to events in America's past.

From its earliest days to the present, Washington has been a setting for history. At the same time, history has shaped the character and appearance of the District of Columbia. Most cities grow and thrive for economic reasons, but Washington is different. After the Revolutionary War, the new American government needed a permanent meeting place. Several northern cities were considered, but Thomas Jefferson and other powerful

A statue of Abraham Lincoln inside the Lincoln Memorial reminds visitors of U.S. history.

George Washington chose the site for the U.S. capital.

southerners did not want a capital in the north. The two sides compromised and decided to build a new city for the capital.

In 1791, President George Washington chose the site for the city that would one day bear his name. He imagined a majestic capital being built on the spot. Andrew Ellicott of Maryland and his assistant, Benjamin Bannecker, a former slave, surveyed a 10-mile (16-kilometer) square of land on both sides of the Potomac. This land contained the early settlements of Georgetown in Maryland and Alexandria in Virginia.

Pierre Charles L'Enfant, a French engineer, was hired to plan the new city. L'Enfant shared the first president's dream, and he planned a city with broad avenues, large parks, and noble buildings. L'Enfant had fought in the American Revolution and believed in the new nation's greatness. Designing its capital became his life's goal.

But in the early years of the United States, Americans did not rush to settle in Washington, D.C. Although the population rose from 3,000 in 1800 to 19,000 by 1830, other cities grew much more rapidly. People found Washington's summer climate uncomfortable. Part of the city was marshland, and disease-carrying mosquitoes were a serious problem. Even Thomas Jefferson called the District of Columbia a "swamp in the wilderness." For more than 70 years, L'Enfant's wide avenues remained muddy and difficult to travel, and cattle and hogs roamed freely in sections of town.

From the beginning, history shaped Washington's appearance. During the War of 1812, British troops set fire to many important buildings, including the White House. James Madison was president at the time. His wife, Dolley, rescued a portrait of George Washington from the flames, but little else could be saved. By 1817, the White House had been rebuilt to the point that James Monroe, who was then president, could move in.

The District of Columbia kept its original boundaries until 1846, when the federal land west of the Potomac was returned to Virginia.

This line drawing shows British soldiers burning Washington, D.C., during the War of 1812.

The city was still so small that no government buildings had been constructed on the Virginia side.

During the 1860s, the Civil War also changed Washington. The capital's location on the Confederate border made it an ideal place for troops to rally before battle and to recover afterward. In the first months of the war, Washington's population rose to more than 100,000 as soldiers and escaped slaves flocked to the city. From 1861 to 1865, while the North fought the South, soldiers were everywhere in Washington, even sleeping in parks and doorways. Spies for both sides roamed the city. Churches became hospitals for the wounded, and the U.S. Capitol served as a laundry and bakery for the troops.

Because Washington's border location meant that it could easily be attacked, forts were built around the city. When Confederate forces did attack just north of Washington, government clerks and other citizens took up weapons to defend the capital.

After the Civil War ended, Americans finally became interested in creating a beautiful capital. People had grown ashamed of Washington's muddy, unfinished condition. With

the government growing, it was time to pave the streets, plant trees, and install water and gas lines. There was a flurry of construction as mansions were built and workers labored on the Library of Congress, the Washington Monument, a new post office building, and other important structures.

The 1900s brought streetcars and automobiles to Washington's roadways, but the new century also brought wars and other difficulties that caused the capital to grow. Thousands of people came to live and work in Washington during World War I. The city's population rose from 330,000 in 1910 to 437,000 just 10 years later.

Another event that changed

Workers labor on the early stages of the Washington Monument. It was begun in 1848 and not finished until 40 years later.

Washington was the Great Depression of the 1930s, a time of hardship across America when many citizens could not find work. As a remedy, President Franklin D. Roosevelt created special programs called the New Deal to give people jobs, protect banks, assist farmers and manufacturers, and help Americans buy homes. The government needed many new workers to make New Deal programs work. These men and women and their families swelled Washington's population. Many new office buildings were constructed, which changed the appearance of the city's downtown area.

Washington has continued to grow. In the 1940s, World War II brought more new workers, homes,

A City for the People

More than any other American city, Washington, D.C., is in the public eye. This city leads two lives—one official, one private. Officially, it is the capital of the United States, the place where laws are made, where news happens, and where the president lives and works each day. In its private life, Washington is the home of about 622,000 Americans and the workplace of many thousands more.

Often visited and frequently photographed, the government's home makes a grand impression. Its wide, tree-lined avenues, white stone buildings, and delicate cherry blossoms are a source of pride for the American people. Many visitors come to the city to enjoy its beauty as they learn about U.S. government and history.

But Washington is more than a collection of monuments and historic

The U.S. Capitol, where the nation's laws are made, rises in the heart of Washington, D.C.

A statue of Thomas Jefferson, one of Washington's many historic sights.

buildings. It is a growing, changing city that can be crowded and noisy with people traveling to work and school. Washington is also an important center of culture, a place where people can watch parades, listen to concerts, and view the work of many artists.

Washington, D.C., is located near the middle of the Atlantic coast, between the states of Maryland and Virginia. It lies on the banks of two rivers, the Potomac River to the west and south, and the Anacostia River to the east. Here, winters are fairly mild, but summers are hot and humid. Most Washingtonians are pleased that heavy snows are uncommon, but when the thermometer reaches the upper 90s, and moisture

Many Washingtonians enjoy sailing or rowing on the Potomac River.

and offices to the city. After 1950, large numbers of black people from the rural south began moving to the District of Columbia in search of equal opportunity and jobs. In fact, the percentage of black residents doubled during this time, and the city became an important center for blacks in many professions.

Life in Washington has always been influenced by the personality and interests of each president. John F. Kennedy's presidency was a time of elegant parties and performances of classical music in the White House. President Lyndon B. Johnson started programs to help the poor in Washington and throughout the country.

Many major events of the past 30 years took place in Washington. In 1963, inspired by the words of Martin Luther King, Jr., more than 200,000 people marched together to demand equal treatment for blacks. That same year, America mourned the death of President Kennedy, who was assassinated in Dallas, Texas; thousands of people filed past his flag-covered coffin in the U.S. Capitol. The death of Martin Luther King, Jr., in 1968 caused violent riots in Washington's streets.

More recently, in 1987, Washington was the first American city visited by Soviet leader Mikhail Gorbachev. It was in Washington that President Ronald Reagan said good-bye to the American people as he finished his eight years in office, and in Washing-

At one time, Washingtonians could not vote to elect their city government officials. Here, Martin Luther King, Jr., *(right)* and others march to support this right.

ton that George Bush was inaugurated as the nation's 41st president.

What will the future hold for the nation's capital? Some residents would like to see the District of Columbia become the 51st American state. Because of its special status, Washington, D.C., does not elect senators and representatives as the 50 states do. Instead, Washingtonians elect one delegate to the House of Representatives who is not permitted to vote on laws. People who want the District of Columbia to become a state believe Washingtonians should be represented as other Americans are. People who disagree think the nation's capital should belong equally to all Americans.

Whether or not it becomes a state, Washington will remain a place where U.S. leaders make decisions that affect all Americans. Today, the city continues to change as businesses move to the area. New office buildings and homes are built, and the suburbs expand. Washingtonians enjoy watching how each new president's concerns affect life in this lively, developing city.

3

The Government at Home

Government and politics are popular topics of conversation in Washington. Not only are so many residents federal employees, but government actions take place practically in their own backyards. Washingtonians find it exciting that the president makes speeches and that laws are passed in the city where they live. To many citizens of Washington, the offices of government are good neighbors who are active in the community's life.

The most famous resident of Washington, D.C., is the president of the United States. The president's home, the White House, is perhaps the one Washington building that most Americans recognize. Visitors to the White House don't see the president at work in the Oval Office, the first lady, or the rooms where they live, but visitors do see the famous portrait of

President Bush at work in the Oval Office.

The historic Red Room.

George Washington that Dolley Madison saved. They can tour the State Dining Room, the historic rooms named for their main colors—the Green Room, Blue Room, and Red Room—as well as the East Room, where President Theodore Roosevelt's children once roller-skated. The East Room is the place where presidential concerts and award ceremonies are often broadcast on national television.

Although the president's office is in the White House, much of the work he oversees is done in the nearby Executive Office Buildings. The president and his staff take part in several holiday celebrations for their Washington neighbors and visitors to the city. Every December, the presi-

Young Washingtonians enjoy the annual Easter egg roll on the White House lawn.

dent lights the giant national Christmas tree on the lawn of the parklike Ellipse near the White House, where people passing by can enjoy its beauty. Each spring, children and their parents gather on the White House lawn for an Easter egg roll.

More than a mile southeast of the White House, at the beginning of Pennsylvania Avenue, stands the U.S. Capitol. Its white dome is another structure that many Americans recognize. The Capitol is the meeting place of the Senate and the House of Representatives, which together form the branch of the government that makes laws.

The senators and representatives meet in large rooms called chambers. These chambers have balconies, known as galleries, where Americans can watch their elected officials debate and vote on new laws. When a vote is about to take place, bells sound throughout the Capitol. In elevators and hallways, everyone must step aside as senators and representatives hurry to take their seats in order to vote.

With 4 acres (1.6 hectares) of floor space, the Capitol also houses paintings and sculpture representing the 50 states and important events in U.S. history. A special subway system connects the Capitol with congressional office buildings just outside the Capitol's grounds.

East of the Capitol lies the Supreme Court, often called "one of the most exciting shows in town." The public may watch from a gallery as the nation's highest court decides whether laws agree with the U.S. Constitution, the document that outlines the government's powers. Supreme Court decisions help shape the laws that everyone in the United States must obey. Sixteen marble columns line the front of the Supreme Court building. They are similar to Greek architecture, to remind people that America's democratic government is based on ideas that began in ancient Greece.

The Supreme Court building.

Some of Washington's most famous residents are not people, but documents. One is the Constitution, and another is the Bill of Rights, which protects the rights of individual Americans. A third is the Declaration of Independence, written when the 13 original colonies declared their freedom from British rule. These documents are displayed in the National Archives Building, within walking distance of the Capitol. The National Archives houses all valuable government records. These three documents

The Declaration of Independence, Constitution, and Bill of Rights are stored in special glass cases in the National Archives.

are so important that they are preserved in heavy glass cases that can be lowered into a vault at night or during emergencies.

Many more documents and books are stored in the Library of Congress, which has a collection so large that it fills not one building, but three. This library holds more than 88 million books, magazines, films, photographs, recordings, and maps, and receives 7,000 new items each day! The Library of Congress is open to the people of the United States. All adults may visit the library to read and study, but books usually cannot be checked out.

Various government offices are clustered around the White House and Capitol, and some of them provide tours to teach the public about the work they do. Many people enjoy touring the Federal Bureau of Investigation, or FBI. The FBI goes to work when federal laws have been broken. The tour allows visitors to watch scientists in crime laboratories working to match fingerprints and uncover clues, and FBI sharpshooters demonstrating their skill. Visitors also see a display of weapons taken from criminals by FBI agents.

The Bureau of Engraving and Printing offers another popular tour, where people can actually see money being made. This government office produces every piece of paper money that Americans use, including dollar bills, postage stamps, and food stamps. Because they handle huge sums of money every day, people who work in the Bureau of Engraving and Printing follow strict security rules. They must keep their lunches, wallets, and other possessions in clear plastic tote bags while they work, and when they leave each day, an officer inspects their purses and briefcases.

In other government offices, many more people work long and hard for the benefit of all Americans. At the main office of the U.S. Postal Service, workers oversee the collection and delivery of more than 100 billion pieces of mail—letters, packages, magazines, and newspapers—every year. Across the Potomac in Arlington, Virginia, is the Pentagon, headquarters of the Defense Depart-

ment. Here, officers in the Army, Navy, Air Force, and Coast Guard remain ready to protect the United States if the need arises. One of the world's largest office buildings, the Pentagon was named for its five-sided shape.

Making the government of the United States of America work requires the efforts of many people. From the president to postal workers, from secretaries to Supreme Court justices, everyone who works for the government has an important job to do. Nowhere are there more U.S. government workers than in the nation's capital, and nowhere is the government more active in community life than in its hometown of Washington, D.C.

A worker inspects newly printed money at the Bureau of Engraving and Printing.

4

The Mall and Beyond

Washington, D.C., is a sightseer's dream. Thanks to L'Enfant's farsighted planning, some of the city's most popular and best-known attractions lie along a 2-mile (3.2-kilometer) stretch of park known popularly as "the Mall." The U.S. Capitol stands on the Mall's east end, facing the Lincoln Memorial on the west end.

On clear, pleasant days, the Mall is a popular spot for noontime joggers, kite flyers, and picnickers. Washingtonians come to the Mall in nice weather to enjoy outdoor concerts and other events; it is an ideal place for picture taking and people watching, as well. Children visiting the Mall might ride a carousel or climb a life-size statue of a dinosaur. Hungry people can buy hot dogs and other snacks from street-side vendors.

Many of the museums that are

The National Mall, with the Lincoln Memorial in the foreground, the Washington Monument in the middle, and the Capitol in the distance.

part of the world-famous Smithsonian Institution are found along the Mall. The Smithsonian is named for James Smithson, a British scientist who so admired the United States that he left his fortune to its government when he died. The U.S. government used Smithson's gift to create what is now the largest group of museums in the world.

The Smithsonian's collections are so large that a visitor could spend an entire day in any one Smithsonian museum and still not see everything it holds. These collections are so varied that they truly contain something for everyone.

The Smithsonian's National Museum of Natural History is the place to learn about all kinds of animal and plant life, and to see dinosaur skeletons and the famous Hope Diamond. Curious children may even hold live caterpillars and cockroaches in the museum's Insect Zoo.

The National Museum of American History, also part of the Smithsonian, houses the flag that was the original Star-Spangled Banner, gowns worn by first ladies beginning with Martha Washington, and everyday items from recent history, such as radios and record players. Archie Bunker's chair from the TV show "All in the Family" and Mr. Rogers's red sweater made headlines when they were added to the collection.

More than 10 million people visit the Smithsonian's National Air and Space Museum every year, making it

Visitors enjoy the exhibits at the National Air and Space Museum, such as this Mercury space capsule.

the world's most popular museum. They come to see the airplanes and spacecraft that hang from the museum's ceiling and fill its vast interior. Visitors can view the airplane the Wright brothers used when they made the first flight, the *Apollo 11* capsule that brought astronauts to the moon, and even a rock brought back from the moon itself! Children and adults alike line up to walk through an actual Skylab spacecraft and scientific laboratory.

The National Gallery of Art, also located on the Mall, contains works by American and foreign artists, past and present. In one room, a red, blue, and black mobile by the American artist Alexander Calder rotates overhead. In another room hangs the only painting in the United States by the great Italian painter and inventor Leonardo da Vinci.

Several of the Smithsonian museums are devoted to art. The doughnut-shaped Hirshhorn Museum and its sculpture garden hold more than 6,500 pieces of modern art. The Arthur M. Sackler Gallery displays Asian art, including delicate jade carvings and modern Chinese paintings. The Museum of African Art is the place to see wooden carved masks and sculptures, and hand-woven decorative cloth.

The Smithsonian's gift shops are an adventure, too. They sell freeze-dried "astronaut" ice cream, copies of paper dolls from long ago, rocks and minerals for collectors, and T-shirts for lovers of nature, science, history, or art.

While the Mall's museums appeal to people's different interests, its monuments bring people together to remember important individuals and events in America's past. At the west end of the Mall are memorials to some of the greatest U.S. presidents and to America's most recent war.

The Washington Monument is the tallest structure in the District of Columbia. Resembling a tall, stone needle, it stands just over 555 feet (169 meters) tall. When it opened for visitors in 1888, the 10-minute elevator ride to the top was a popular attraction. Today that ride takes only 70 seconds. From the top, visitors get

The Washington Monument, framed by cherry blossoms.

a bird's-eye view of the city in four directions.

The Washington Monument rises near one end of a long pool called the Reflecting Pool. At the other end is a temple-like building where a statue of President Abraham Lincoln sits facing the city. Many visitors walk up the 56 steps of the Lincoln Memorial to view the thoughtful, seated statue of the leader who worked hard to preserve the United States during the Civil War. On the inside walls of the monument are carved two of Lincoln's best-remembered speeches, the Gettysburg Address and the Second Inaugural Address.

South of the other monuments, in a beautiful spot overlooking the Tidal Basin, stands the memorial to the third U.S. president, Thomas Jefferson. Known as the author of the Declaration of Independence, Jefferson was also an architect. His memorial is famous for its dome and columns, two of his favorite architectural features. The Jefferson Memorial is especially pretty in spring, when the many surrounding cherry trees are in bloom.

The newest memorial on the Mall honors the Americans who fought in the Vietnam War. Often called "the Wall," the Vietnam Veterans Memorial consists of two black granite walls, together almost 500 feet (152.5 meters) long. The names of more than 50,000 Americans killed or missing in the war are

The white-domed Jefferson Memorial.

Visitors come to the Vietnam Veterans Memorial to remember the many Americans who served in this war.

carved into its polished surface. Many visitors are moved to tears by the Wall, and they often leave flowers or other items in memory of the people they loved.

The Mall is linked to other parts of the city by Washington's under-

ground train system, called the Metro. Train lines named for colors— blue, orange, red, yellow—connect city and suburban neighborhoods. The system is still being built, and soon the green line will be added.

From the Mall, the Metro rumbles under the Potomac River. One of its stops, Arlington National Cemetery, is the resting place of about 60,000 Americans who served their country in war. Several government officials and heroes are buried in Arlington. Here can be seen the grave of President John F. Kennedy, with its eternal flame, a fire that is always kept burning. Also buried here are the president's brother, Senator Robert F. Kennedy, and Washington's planner, Pierre Charles L'Enfant. Visitors often stop at the Tomb of the Unknowns, which honors all Americans who died in war.

Washington is famous for lively places as well as serious ones. One of the busiest is the John F. Kennedy Center for the Performing Arts,

The John F. Kennedy Center for the Performing Arts.

located on the banks of the Potomac just northwest of the Lincoln Memorial. Almost every day of the year, artists perform concerts, plays, operas, and ballets at the Kennedy Center. The center has three main theaters and regularly presents programs for children. The Kennedy Center is called a "living memorial" because it was built both to honor a past president and to be used by the American people.

The National Zoo is always bustling, too. Roomy and wooded, the zoo offers the opportunity to see some unusual animals. It houses the United States' only giant pandas—a gift to the American people from the People's Republic of China—as well as other endangered animals, such as polar bears, bald eagles, and pygmy hippopotamuses. Children who visit the zoo enjoy its "hands-on" exhibits, including Birdlab, where they can learn about birds by handling feathers, nests, and eggs.

Sightseeing in Washington is not expensive, because places of interest that are owned by the government charge no admission. The Smithsonian, the monuments, even the zoo— all are free. These attractions are supported by people's taxes and maintained for everyone's benefit. In a sense, they belong to all Americans.

A giant panda, the most famous resident of the National Zoo.

5

Washington's Neighborhoods

The city of Washington was planned with the U.S. Capitol at its heart. Although the Capitol is not the actual center of Washington, it is still the point people use to describe direction in the city. Washington addresses are said to be northwest, northeast, southwest, or southeast, according to where they lie in relation to the Capitol.

There are no skyscrapers or high-rise apartment houses in Washington, D.C. Tall buildings are not allowed by law so that the Washington Monument will always be the tallest structure in the city. As a result, instead of growing upward as many cities do, Washington has grown outward.

At times when the city's population grew—especially during the Great Depression and the two World Wars—more living space was needed. As old neighborhoods filled, people

Washington, D.C., is a carefully planned city, known for features such as this traffic circle with its park in the middle.

The vice-president's house. Washington is known for its many beautiful, expensive homes.

built new homes and towns in the surrounding countryside. Today the growth continues, reaching out into the suburbs in Maryland and Virginia.

The cost of housing has shaped the city, too. Washington's homes are among the most expensive in the nation. Many families need two incomes, and many Washington mothers work outside the home—the highest percentage in the country. Even with two parents working, a house can be difficult to afford. Often, families must rent rather than own their homes.

Today's Washington is a city where modern communities surround old, historic neighborhoods. It is home to wealthy people, poor people, and a large middle class. Yet, new or old, elegant or run-down, Washington's neighborhoods change with time.

Some of the people who help neighborhoods change are called "urban pioneers." These people buy old houses that need repairs, usually in poor neighborhoods. Then they begin fixing their homes, making them clean and beautiful again. Urban pioneers might do this because it is the only way they can afford to own a house in the city, or because they want to save a historic place from ruin.

One place that has been changed by hard work is Georgetown, one of Washington's oldest neighborhoods. It is located in northwest Washington, about a mile (1.6 kilometers) from the White House. Seventy years ago, Georgetown's residents were poor, and its historic houses were falling down. Today, Georgetown is a fashionable home to some of Washington's wealthiest citizens. The old row houses that line Georgetown's cobblestone streets have been restored and are now colorfully painted and well tended.

The hard work that saved Georgetown is now bringing new life to other Washington neighborhoods. One such place is Capitol Hill, located just east of the U.S. Capitol.

Colorfully painted rowhouses line a street in Georgetown.

Here, streets lined with luxurious homes and marble government buildings lie next to blocks of run-down houses. Yet, elegant or shabby, almost anyplace in the neighborhood offers a great view of the Capitol dome.

Like all cities, Washington faces the problems of poverty, both in Capitol Hill and elsewhere. Thousands of poor, black citizens live in neighborhoods such as Anacostia, part of the city's southeast section across the Anacostia River from the Mall. Here, many residents are without jobs or decent houses and must cope with high rates of street crime and drug abuse. As drug abuse has spread, the number of murders in the District of Columbia has been rising sharply. In fact, the city now has the

Choir members from Washington's Eastern High School showed a drive to succeed.

highest murder rate in the country. Law enforcement experts believe that many of these deaths result from fights between drug dealers.

Some young Washingtonians in poor neighborhoods may be tempted to use drugs, commit crimes, or join street gangs, but others are struggling to succeed. In 1988, the choir from Eastern High School, located in a poor area near Capitol Hill, placed second in the International Youth and Music Festival in Vienna, Austria. The choir members practiced four hours a day for this difficult competition, and they raised most of the money to pay for their trip. President Reagan expressed the city's pride in these young people by inviting them to perform at the White House.

Some Washington neighborhoods are home to people of different backgrounds. The residents of Adams-Morgan, in northwest Washington, boast about their mixed community of middle class and poor, white and black, Hispanic and Asian citizens. The foods and traditions of these different groups have made Columbia Road, Adams-Morgan's main street, a popular place to meet. Many Washingtonians come here to eat in Adams-Morgan's varied restaurants, where they can sample African dishes such as cous cous and Hispanic favorites such as paella, chorizo, and black bean soup. Each September, the community hosts Adams-Morgan Day, a celebration with loud, lively music and Hispanic, African, and Asian foods.

Not far from Adams-Morgan is another neighborhood with an international feeling. Along the stretch of Massachusetts Avenue called Embassy Row are the offices that represent the governments of foreign countries in the United States. Many of these embassies are mansions that were once the homes of wealthy families. Most embassies display their countries' names on their gates or doorways, as well as their national

The Embassy of Egypt is one of many foreign embassies lining Massachusetts Avenue.

flags. The foreign diplomats and their families join other Washingtonians to shop, attend school, and see the many sights the city has to offer.

Residents in all of Washington's neighborhoods share interests that make them feel like part of one large community. Many are fans of the Redskins football team. The Redskins are so popular in Washington that when they won the Super Bowl in 1988, President Reagan gave federal employees time off from work to watch

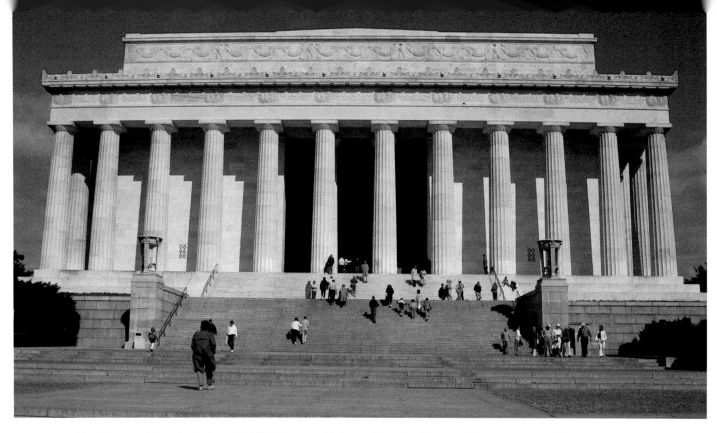

The famous historical places in Washington, D.C., such as the Lincoln Memorial, help Washingtonians feel a tie to the nation's past, present, and future.

their victory parade through the city.

People from different neighborhoods also like to spend time in Rock Creek Park, a wooded strip of land stretching north from the National Zoo into suburban Maryland. Here, they can spend a day outdoors on the park's many hiking trails, observe wildlife in its nature center, or learn about the nighttime sky in its planetarium.

Washingtonians enjoy the many festivals that take place in their city. The popular Festival of American

Folklife is held on the Mall each summer. This festival features country and bluegrass music, and gives people the opportunity to watch artists make typical American handicrafts.

Residents in all of Washington's neighborhoods share a concern about the problems of poverty, crime, and drug abuse that their city faces. At the same time, they recognize the many benefits of living in the U.S.

capital. They feel a special tie to America's past and are proud to share their community with the United States government and to host the many visitors who come to the District of Columbia each year. Living in the nation's capital presents risks and challenges, but it also provides excitement and opportunity. Many Washingtonians wouldn't have it any other way.

Places to Visit in Washington, D.C.

Smithsonian Museums

The following buildings are part of the Smithsonian:

Arts and Industries Building
900 Jefferson Drive, SW
Houses many objects originally displayed at the Philadelphia Exhibition of 1876

Hirshhorn Museum and Sculpture Garden
Independence Avenue at 6th Street, SW

National Air and Space Museum
Independence Avenue and 7th Street, SW

National Museum of African Art
950 Independence Avenue, SW

National Museum of American Art
8th and G streets, NW

National Museum of American History
Constitution Avenue at 13th Street, NW

National Museum of Natural History
Constitution Avenue at 10th Street, NW

National Portrait Gallery
8th and F streets, NW
Displays portraits of U.S. presidents and famous Americans

Renwick Gallery
Pennsylvania Avenue at 17th Street, NW
Exhibits of crafts, design, and the decorative arts

Arthur M. Sackler Gallery of Art
1050 Independence Avenue, SW

For more information on the Smithsonian, call or write:

Smithsonian Institution
Visitors Information and Associates Reception Center
1000 Jefferson Drive, SW
Washington, DC 20560
(202) 357-2700

Other Museums

Capital Children's Museum
800 3rd Street, NE
(202) 543-8600
Interactive exhibits about science, history, and culture

Corcoran Gallery
17th Street at New York Avenue, NW
(202) 638-3211
A privately supported museum dedicated to displaying American art

Dolls' House and Toy Museum
5236 44th Street, NW
(202) 244-0024
Exhibits of antique dolls, dollhouses, and toys

National Gallery of Art
Constitution Avenue and 6th Street, NW
(West Wing)
Constitution Avenue and 4th Street, NW
(East Wing)
(202) 737-4215 (general information)
(202) 842-6249 (children's tours and family programs)

Washington Navy Yard, Navy Memorial Museum
9th and M streets, SE
(202) 433-2651
Exhibits cover the history of the navy from the Revolutionary War to the present; visitors can tour a navy destroyer

Monuments and Memorials

Jefferson Memorial
Tidal Basin, West Potomac Park, SW
(202) 485-9666

Lincoln Memorial
The Mall at 23rd Street, NW
(202) 485-9666

Vietnam Veterans Memorial
21st Street and Constitution Avenue, NW
(202) 485-9666

Washington Monument
The Mall at 15th Street, NW
(202) 485-9666

U.S. Government Buildings

Bureau of Engraving and Printing
14th Street at C Street, SW
(202) 447-9709

Library of Congress
Thomas Jefferson Building
1st and East Capitol streets, SE
(202) 707-6400

Federal Bureau of Investigation
Pennsylvania Avenue between 9th and 10th
streets, NW
(202) 324-3000

National Archives and Records Admin-
istration
7th Street at Pennsylvania Avenue, NW
(202) 523-3000

Supreme Court of the United States
1st and East Capitol streets, NW
(202) 479-3000

United States Capitol
Capitol Hill
(202) 225-6827

White House
1600 Pennsylvania Avenue, NW
(202) 456-7041

Special Places

Arlington National Cemetery
Arlington, Virginia
(703) 692-0931

Dumbarton Oaks
R Street at 32nd Street, NW
(202) 338-8278
*Once a private home, this mansion features an
art collection and landscaped gardens*

Dumbarton House
2715 Q Street, NW
(202) 337-2288
A restored house of the colonial period

Ford's Theatre
511 10th Street, NW
(202) 426-6924

John F. Kennedy Center for the Performing
Arts
New Hampshire Avenue and F Street, NW
(202) 254-3600

National Aquarium
14th Street between E Street and Constitution Avenue, NW
(202) 377-2825
*The nation's oldest aquarium, containing more
than 1,000 specimens*

National Geographic Society
17th and M streets, NW
(202) 857-7000
Changing exhibits on geography, anthropology, photography, history, and scientific pursuits

National Zoological Park
3001 Connecticut Avenue, NW
(202) 673-4800

Rock Creek Park
5000 Glover Road, NW
(202) 426-6828

Union Station
50 Massachusetts Avenue, NE
(202) 682-0079
Washington's railroad station was recently restored; it contains many interesting shops and a food hall

Additional information can be obtained from:

Washington Convention and Visitors Association
1455 Pennsylvania Avenue, NW
Washington, DC 20004
(202) 692-2788

Washington, D.C.:   A Historical Time Line

1789   Georgetown University is founded

1790   The U.S. Congress decides that a permanent American capital should be built on the banks of the Potomac River

1791   George Washington acquires the land for the new city

1800   The government moves from Philadelphia, its temporary home, to Washington, D.C.

1802   The first local elections for city government are held in Washington, D.C.

1814   British troops set fire to Washington's buildings, including the White House

1817   President James Monroe moves into the rebuilt White House

1846   The portion of the District of Columbia west of the Potomac River is returned to Virginia; the Smithsonian Institution is established

1848   The cornerstone of the Washington Monument is laid

1861   The Civil War begins; thousands of soldiers arrive in Washington

1864   The first soldier is buried in the new military cemetery in Arlington, Virginia

1865   President Abraham Lincoln is assassinated in Ford's Theatre

1874   The U.S. Congress takes away Washingtonians' right to elect local government officials; the city is run by a three-member commission appointed by the president

1888   The Washington Monument opens for visitors

1917   The United States enters World War I; thousands of new workers move to Washington, D.C.

1922   The Lincoln Memorial is completed

1932   Franklin D. Roosevelt is elected president; he establishes his New Deal program, which creates many new jobs in Washington, D.C.

1935   The Supreme Court moves into its present quarters

1941   The United States enters World War II; again, the government work force in Washington expands

1942   The Jefferson Memorial is completed

1943   The Pentagon is built as headquarters for the U.S. Defense Department

1963   Approximately 200,000 people march on Washington, asking for civil rights for blacks; President John F. Kennedy is buried in Arlington National Cemetery

1964   Washingtonians vote in presidential elections for the first time

1968   Riots break out in the city following the news that the Reverend Martin Luther King, Jr., has been shot

1970   For the first time in almost 100 years, Washingtonians are allowed to elect a non-voting representative to the U.S. House of Representatives

1971   The John F. Kennedy Center for the Performing Arts opens

1973   Washingtonians are given the right to elect city government officials

1976   The Smithsonian's National Air and Space Museum opens to the public

1982   The movement to make the District of Columbia a state grows in popularity; a constitution is written and submitted to Congress

1987   Soviet leader Mikhail Gorbachev and his wife, Raisa Gorbachev, visit Washington, D.C.

1989   George Bush is sworn in as the 41st president of the United States

The Presidents of the United States

President	Years in Office	President	Years in Office
George Washington	1789-1797	Chester A. Arthur	1881-1885
John Adams	1797-1801	Grover Cleveland	1885-1889 1893-1897
Thomas Jefferson	1801-1809	Benjamin Harrison	1889-1893
James Madison	1809-1817	William McKinley	1897-1901
James Monroe	1817-1825	Theodore Roosevelt	1901-1909
John Quincy Adams	1825-1829	William Howard Taft	1909-1913
Andrew Jackson	1829-1837	Woodrow Wilson	1913-1921
Martin Van Buren	1837-1841	Warren G. Harding	1921-1923
William Henry Harrison	1841	Calvin Coolidge	1923-1929
John Tyler	1841-1845	Herbert Hoover	1929-1933
James K. Polk	1845-1849	Franklin D. Roosevelt	1933-1945
Zachary Taylor	1849-1850	Harry S. Truman	1945-1953
Millard Fillmore	1850-1853	Dwight D. Eisenhower	1953-1961
Franklin Pierce	1853-1857	John F. Kennedy	1961-1963
James Buchanan	1857-1861	Lyndon B. Johnson	1963-1969
Abraham Lincoln	1861-1865	Richard M. Nixon	1969-1974
Andrew Johnson	1865-1869	Gerald R. Ford	1974-1977
Ulysses S. Grant	1869-1877	James E. Carter, Jr.	1977-1981
Rutherford B. Hayes	1877-1881	Ronald Reagan	1981-1989
James A. Garfield	1881	George Bush	1989-

Index